The Thunder and Lightning Men

By Becky Gold

Illustrated by Bradley Clark

Scott Foresman
is an imprint of

PEARSON

Glenview, Illinois • Boston, Massachusetts • Chandler, Arizona •
Upper Saddle River, New Jersey

Illustrations
Bradley Clark.

ISBN 13: 978-0-328-51387-1
ISBN 10:   0-328-51387-3

11 12 13 14   V0FL 17 16 15 14

Did you ever wonder how thunder and lightning came to be? A Passamaquoddy (pas uh muh KWAHD ee) legend gives one explanation. Listen as the narrator tells the story….

Once, a man was caught up in a roaring thunderstorm and carried far away to the village of the thunders. The thunder and lightning men lived there. They carried bows and arrows like actual men, but they also had wings with which they could fly.

The chief of the thunder and lightning men called them together, for it was time to fly. He told the winged men where to go and how long to be gone.

"Do not fly too low," he warned. "If you do, you may get caught in the trees."

The man watched, amazed, as the thunder and lightning men took off, whirling and soaring overhead. He wondered how they had been chosen to be thunder and lightning men.

The chief then turned to the stranger and greeted him kindly. He asked the man if he wanted to become a thunder and lightning man too. Excitedly the man said yes. He wanted to fly overhead with wings as he had seen the others do.

"In that case," said the chief, "we will need to have a ceremony. Are you ready?" the chief asked.

"I am," said the man.

"Then let the ceremony begin," said the chief.

First, the chief brought out a large box. The man stepped into it, and it was locked up tight. Then the man lost all of his senses. He could not see. He could not smell. He could not hear or feel anything around him.

When he finally stepped out of the box, the man was given a pair of wings and a bow and arrow. He became like one of the thunder and lightning men, and that made him happy. He flew with them on their many journeys.

Where did they go? They flew to the south, or *sou' n' snouk*, a land of other languages. They flew over the southern mountains, causing powerful storms.

The man behaved like his companions. He poked the earth with arrows of lightning. The lightning would burst as it touched the ground. He beat his wings, making a thunderous noise. The noise would echo off the mountain walls and fill the air. He enjoyed making the earth shake and tremble.

One of the things the thunder and lightning men liked to do most was hunt the thunderbird. This beautiful creature lived in the southern mountains. The men searched for her high and low. Sometimes they would only catch a quick peek of her. They were always hoping to shoot the thunderbird. But that is what they were never able to do. She was much faster than they were. Even when they thought they were close to getting her, she easily escaped.

The thunder and lightning men also loved to play ball. They would throw and hit a ball all over the sky, laughing and having fun. The man liked playing with the others. He'd never imagined that he would play ball while flying up in the clouds! He knew he was seeing and doing things that most people only dreamed of. He wondered if the other thunder and lightning men knew this too.

The man stayed in the land of the thunder and lightning men for a long time. He liked having wings and flying around the sky with his companions. He was almost one of them. Still, something wasn't quite right. After a while, he began to tire a little of all the flying and fun. He remembered things from his old life. He kept thinking of all the things that he missed.

He thought about a time one fall when he went hunting in the woods near his village. He spied a large buck with great antlers moving through the trees. Slowly and carefully, he aimed his bow and arrow and shot it. After that, he held a huge feast for the entire village. It was a time of joy spent with family and friends. It was a pleasant memory.

He thought about his wife and his three small children. One was only a baby when he had left. He remembered playing with his children and teaching his sons. Tears came to his eyes as he pictured them.

He realized that he missed his family very much. Surely they missed him too. The man knew that they must be wondering where he was and when he was coming back.

The day came when the man felt that he was ready to burst with longing. He could not bear to be away from his family anymore. He went to the chief with a sad heart. He knew it was time for him to leave the thunder and lightning men.

"I miss my family," he said to the chief. "I am ready to leave. I want to go home."

The chief nodded. "Then now is the time for you to go," he said kindly.

Calling all his men together, the chief explained what the man had told him. He asked the thunder and lightning men to bring the man back to his home.

The thunder and lightning men reluctantly did the chief's bidding. They did not like to see their friend go. They had come to think of the man as their brother.

Thunder roared. Lightning clashed. Soon the people of the man's village thought they saw something shaped like a man coming through the sky. They couldn't believe their eyes!

They all began talking excitedly. Soon they understood who it was coming toward them. It was a man! It was their tribesman, who had been gone seven long years. He was home at last, and what stories he had to tell!

The Passamaquoddy

The Passamaquoddy people traditionally lived in the coastal areas of Maine and New Brunswick, Canada. They hunted and fished for their living and made beautiful birch bark canoes, baskets, and other crafts. Today the Passamaquoddy's tribal government is in the state of Maine.

Passamaquoddy legends tell that the thunder and lightning were actually spirits that they could see. The lightning was the fire and smoke of their pipes. They also believed there was a "thunder bullet" that these spirits leave behind.

A Passamaquoddy birch bark canoe

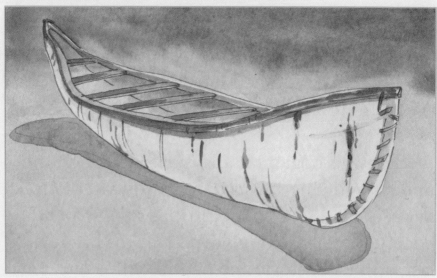